Generous Peril

Alan Elyshevitz

Cyberwit.net
HIG 45 Kaushambi Kunj, Kalindipuram
Allahabad - 211011 (U.P.) India
http://www.cyberwit.net
Tel: +(91) 9415091004
E-mail: info@cyberwit.net

Printed at Repro India Limited.

Contents

My Wife Is Shrinking

Lately, my wife has been shrinking.
She speaks of bone density, of her spine
transforming into brittle April ice.

She knows there are many ways to diminish:
mental disease, freak accident, brutal attack.
Our affluence, she tells me, is manufactured
by addled workmen chained to machines
whose sharp protrusions and blind moving parts
slice the flesh of the nearest available soul.

Of this she has read, heard, and exchanged
ideas. Messages have been written, sent,
and received expressing proactive intentions.

Calcium, however, remains a problem:
its insufficiency. Soon, she jokes, she will be
small enough to be carried in her own purse
in which she keeps the ghost of a pet Airedale
and a photo of her father wearing a chef's hat,
not to mention the aforementioned affluence.

While those workmen lose their fingers or
dive into toxic vats to escape beatings or
snag on wires at remote border crossings,

stature becomes increasingly urgent.
My wife must do something, she says,
to appease her vertebrae before it's too late.

She takes medication that tastes
like chalk, like soap, like the despair
inherent in retail hair dye. Meanwhile,

those desiccated workmen have fled
into a wilderness of combustible trees
where ravens pester their dignity.

My wife applies her stalwart mind
to the problem. She packs binoculars,
lunch, and a fire extinguisher and goes
bird watching, but the birds watch her
grow ever smaller until a raven swoops in
and rips the field guide from her tiny hands.

Late Summer

More and more, I notice your gravity,
a melancholy tilt toward the equator.
In the backyard you wring out deplorable
bath towels and discard infested cornflakes
while the sun maligns the tender acreage
in the middle of your life. September evenings
undermine the finest constellations and incite
the downfall of fireflies. Beyond the lawn
and our lopsided fence, you take my hand
as we churn through piles of anathema
expelled from the treetops. I want to suggest
tricyclics or some other panacea from my lofty
thesaurus. I want to know why you've paid
a manicurist to truncate your fingernails.

Lot's Wife

for Anna Akhmatova

Autumn is surely the crust of the year,
Its pieces scattered for chickens that
Lurch like matrons with cranky hips.
Anna, you are understandably morose

In a nation of fried and boiled meat.
In the pantry of your cottage in exile,
Old potatoes have the obstinate eyes
And callous skin of your ex-husband.

Outside, the cackle of falling leaves may be
White noise or the very message you desire.
Meanwhile, for dinner you dream of foie gras
And a smuggled morsel of hope from the city

Of your sentiments. By morning the coop may
Produce a few eggs which some say contain the
Biographies of martyrs, for they taste unbearably
Sublime when accompanied by a pillar of salt.

Hurricane

*A wind of such violence / Will tolerate no bystanding: I must
shriek*   Sylvia Plath, "Elm"

Here comes the storm of the century again,
more profound this time than a dewdrop

It is our affliction of the moment,
a bad headline for anxious eyes

A wrecked ambulance appears radiant
and lurid bedecked in toppled phone lines

The car horns, the embarrassed medical
team, the fluids bursting from every sewer

In public shelters the dispossessed cough
into their hands like guttering candles

How they yield to the deepening blackout,
jostle, compete, exchange ingratitudes

There is no refastening dislodged pride
nor the limbs of any man or tree

A swath of humiliated poplars extends
all the way to the high countryside

Vegetables rest in their easy valor,
their noses deep in fragrant mud

To be a squat dense thing — resilient,
wrapped in leaves, optimistic, home

The Donor

I do not know what is wrong
with me. Once I see, I cannot
un-see. This must be an electrical
phenomenon. Though distracted
by diagnostic imagery, I view
my contusions as blossoms of mishap.

Upon this table I seem gallant
somehow, instrumental. I must trust
the professionals, for my skin feels
abstract. Still, I wish they would blow
on their gloves before touching me.

They are cutting now, extracting
pieces to arrange on a cotton towel.
I am awed by such fastidious acts,
mistaking them for signs of reverence.

I feel boredom and wonder concurrently
in this silver silence and silver light.
In this faint life of mine, I recall a dog
not my own, a twisted window screen,
and pavement slick with heavy rain.

Now they decamp with what
crowded me. The light slackens
like a loosened necktie. Two doors
knit themselves shut. Within hours
my lungs will engulf other air.
By dawn my heart will beat elsewhere.

Geriatrics

At the end of the tunnel
　　I see no light
So lenses are fitted
　　to bend my vision
Read this with one eye
　　now the other
But the inner eye blurs
　　from age and prescription

The blood pressure band is pumped and pumped
　　yet a vein cannot be found to puncture
The body's complaints are professional mourners
　　who will not be consoled

The doctors and nurses are young in this clinic
　　snappy as pop tunes
brimming with dreams of income
　　They warn me to limit
my intake of fluids
　　abstain from salt
They do not view this life
　　as a desert — a landscape
　　seventy years in the making
They wile away in the crisp oasis
　　sipping miraculous tea
　　as I stagger toward the final dune
　　dying of thirst

Enemy

Look for his well-trained beard in aerial
photographs of a bunker dispelled
by bombardment. Sift through the rumors

of his guile: he is the anonymous larynx
in a steep minaret; the elderly gentleman,
robust and flamboyant, on line for a ferry;

the shepherd, the tortoise, the utility knife.
Though Bosnian he speaks with a Farsi
inflection. He owns a gift shop in Hamburg

and nurtures the grounds of a swank
Indonesian resort. In private he smokes.
In intimate company he sips esoteric tea.

With protozoan cunning he splits,
he divides. He takes an elevator
to an unnumbered floor. His suit and tie

fully memorized, he knocks on a door
with just the right force. He's got his story
straight, and he's prepared to turn us in.

Pockets

When he died his heirs discovered an accumulation
in his clothes: in a left pants pocket a torn belt loop
and a lozenge embittered by lint, in the right
a coin with the face of a dehydrated president.

From a back pocket—the one without a wallet—
they extracted a shy ticket stub. An old suit
contained an invitation to an empire's collapse,
an expired analgesic, and a steadfast comb.

From an oversized robe they dislodged, with effort,
a sleepless night that inspired his preoccupied mind.
From a leather jacket they set free an American
highway parallel to a longer, more scenic route.

At last they removed each item from the pocket
nearest his heart: a crushed pine cone,
an unattached button, a charred ambition.

La Tienda Mexicana

Joaquin has been told to drive slowly.
Beside the highway, where the climate's hips
have enlarged, various grains and pollinators
give way to desert and spacious flies.
In the mountains he comes from, three men
are dead, yet the avalanche continues
with its hard loose teeth. Just as the wind
has teeth. And dogs on guard at warehouse gates.
Brownfields are safe to pull over and sleep
while the Earth plots schisms within itself.
In the morning he awakens to entropy,
his eyelashes spiked and brittle. At 6 AM
in a sales-pitch town, he meets idle men
flexing their knuckles. There's a restaurant job
he's reluctant to take because kitchen blades
brush onions aside, probing for thumbs.
Joaquin values his hands too much,
especially fingertips once kissed
by homeland beauty. He drives slowly
past derelict ladders, half-hung windows.
It's December in a posh warm-weather region.
Never, he thinks, will he know hypothermia
or be fitted for a homeowner's loan.
Hunger climbs from the trench in his gut.
Joaquin has been told to obtain what he needs
from the Mexican store. To save money
he chooses to gnaw on whatever happens next.

Akhmatova #4

I owe you succor, greenery, sap
And crickets. On your messy
Knees, reasons and thumbtacks
Have left their marks.

It's my fault, Anna. I didn't
Keep kosher nor tune your ukulele.
And when I opened the door to the tropics,
Your cat wandered off in the snow.

Forgive me: for shifting the waters,
For diverting the salmon from sex
Galore, for hoarding the river
In a block of ice.

Akhmatova #6

The saints seem to budget their answers
To prayers. You'd think otherwise,
With their loyalty oaths and all those
Crowns bestowed on hemophiliacs.

And with such impressive c.v.'s
Of simony and illuminated manuscripts
And cathedrals that fell through
The floor of mathematics.

Anna, your prayers are too far-reaching
For saints whose bones a priest lets you
Kiss for ten zloty in Poland
Or fifteen francs in southern France.

Take the gold, Anna, or the mate who
Quits drinking, or the infant with ten
Working fingers. Smile at the priest
And walk away.

Akhmatova #10

At each red light, the Cambodian cabbie skims
his dictionary, mouthing words — *advance, rascal.*
In the back seat, your lover fingers a catalog
of leather belts. Your lover loves boundaries
(starched cuffs, tapered shirts),
his wardrobe as nifty as a lawsuit.

Three blocks from your apartment —
equivalent, phantasm — your lover sees
his image in the passenger window with a real
flower bed across the street cushioning his head.
But a magnificent tulip is, to him, a mere death wish.
And he prefers the immutable sales tax
for which he always carries spare change.

Bilious, target — Your lover has arrived.
"Did you know," he remarks to the cabbie,
"that tigers in Asia are nearly extinct?"
The driver smiles for a generous tip;
your lover smiles for reasons less worthy.

Now your lover is climbing your staircase,
which he views as a metaphor, his cachet
ascending to the climax of your bed.
Anna, you have access to a real fire escape.
Repeat after me — *metallic, ladder, descend.*

Kaddish

for Rose Dorn

May His Great Name be sanctified
by the sweet cheap sodas
you bought me and my brothers
from the laundromat vending machine
along with forbidden diner BLT's
created according to His will. *Omein*

Blessed, praised, glorified, exalted, extolled,
honored, elevated, lauded —
His Name and your name,
and the one name you called us —
"Sweetie" this, "Sweetie" that —
for you could never remember
your grandchildren's names.

Blessings, hymns, praise, consolation
for the grease monkeys half your age
who flirted with you at the Olds dealership
where you kept the books upon which
all of them suckled. *Omein*

Why, after selling our grandfather's car,
did you live in front of the Magnavox
with the twisted antenna that snared
Guy Lombardo on New Year's Eve
while you sniffed your dead husband's
dead smoke rings?

Why did you never marry after 1959?
This is His secret, His secret and yours,
which you carried with you to the Bingo hall,
to the diner and the laundromat,
to successful hip surgery
and not so successful treatment of
heart
bladder
spleen
skin
heart
kidneys
heart
lungs
heart heart heart

Blessed be the white wisps of your hair
and the coma that subdued your fear —
that ugly tube-tied restfulness
that masquerades as death. *Omein*

Now that you rest in your House of Israel
made of pine, we stand with a sweating rabbi
and his minion of flies in the crux of summer,
dust in our collars, rivers in our palms,
the dry taste of prayer on our lips.

Yis'ga'dal v'yis'kadash
The least we can do
is stand for you, stand
forever and ever. *Omein*

Amanuensis

Tell me, Uncle, about Japan during that lucky
hiatus between war and titanium. Tell me about
your stickball soldiery and how the people loved
bird art and natural light on their gardens and fish plates.
Tell me about the Tenryû and what the typhoon did
to Osaka Bay, how a raindrop capsized unstable land
and you couldn't help but notice the flood-proof eyes
of "girlfriends" in photos your comrades sent home.
Tell me, Uncle, about Private Something from Colorado
who bunked in amplitude modulation right next to you
in the barracks. How he, who relished the integral sex
of engorgement, kept you awake like a Cuban rumor,
kept you up in the dark as though you had been here
breathing the husky air after the first or second bomb.

New Jersey, or Somewhere

We've returned for a day of nostalgia and nativist
ice cream. So old is our old town that it curates a myth
of patriots. Still standing, we find, the high school
of blackface but with many more parking restrictions.
The generic avenue paved with alluvial grit is one reason
the soles of our feet need a buffer. At lunch in a tavern
of extinct smells, a mixologist takes whiskey and bacon
to the next level with an infusion of materials science.
True, we leave a little high. The old highway surmounts
a ravine where precision stitching resolves into railroad
and a river just lying there. Only the highlands still
exist for studying the deep digestion of trees. And
in the lowlands, the state remains adamant about its
cranberry marsh while deer look on with metallic wounds.

The Engine

Tutoring me on the parts
of this engine you lull me
to sleep like religion
The mysteries of manifold wires
and the holy blood called lubricant
you honor as if the souls
of our forebears
inhabit the cylinders

Who are those icy men and women
in the old photographs
in your dresser drawer?
What made that childhood scar
between your fingers?

When you summon me
to feel where a hose leads
I twist my graduation ring
round and round on my finger
to coax some talent from my hands
while things we won't speak of
hum in the background
running on inexhaustible fuel

Another Fraudulent Memoir

When I was a boy, rat poison was a quaint way out
of bankruptcy. On the other hand, pills, an amateur
trigger finger, a lengthy submergence in a lukewarm
bath. From my sickbed, I heard the clouds cough and roll
over on their sides while my mother regulated biochemical
traffic. In my hometown, a baseball that once belonged
to my father molted its hide in a forgotten corner of an empty
lot. Perhaps a genetic predisposition prompted us to measure
time by means of expedient needles. Still, there was no
dependable calculus between the dead robin in our birdbath
and the filthy dishes wading in the sink. Deprived of
a passport, I believed in family. Eventually, I recovered.

Parochial Sonnet

The schoolyard fence: its upright hubris. My fingers
—or some other boy's—pulled wretched music
from chain links. They kept us separate from the girls
to observe the alphas rise, and pressed us until space
was left for only noses to run. "Dago," they called me.
In black they kneeled me to a shadow of myself.
The nuns assembled within an architecture none of us
could penetrate. Some of us, risking shatter, longed
through windows for a bigtime landscape beyond
the fruit juice, watered down. We soon lost our edges
and muscle tone. This education, like a morbid fracture,
never healed quite right. In those days my father was a prince
of asbestos who lived with a growth on his bladder.
I'm all prayed out, he said to me. *Now, God leaves me alone.*

Habitat

I was raised on an island of rotting jetties. The county
did all it could to customize a stretch for babies' feet.
Still, the beach was spiked with half-shelled clams
relieved of their persecuted meat. We had fun
with eyelash diffraction as we dragged umbrellas
in the sand. At times we stopped to catch the scent
of bait on each other's arms or notice blue epoxy
clinging to the sky. When older we slept among
the bottles until we exhausted rebates from the sun.
No, my world is not yet an ingot. Marbled it remains
by gravitational tides. But the county's protective fencing
of dunes and shorebird habitat has undergone opprobrious
collapse. Centimeters north of my sexagenarian brow,
pathogens probe for weakness in a barrier of blood.

Impression: Sunday

How it feels: like a residue of sand
in a tennis shoe or the pressure
of a half-inflated bicycle tire.

The barbecue grills churn
out the smoky aromas
of instinct and destiny.

We hunker down with cheese-
flavored dip, the last cans of soda,
and our turbulent stomachs.

For the last time, the stoical
among us stand erect, waiting
to vanish like old-growth cedar.

Death by Pizza

Everybody knows it's bad for you: the saturation, the very
weight, like burial in lipid cement. The delivery boy,
as hysterical as a bad day in Jerusalem, can't make change.
When I tell him to keep it all, a jack-o-lantern grin imperils his face.

I hear a cat retching in the shrubbery. A wildfire ignited with
a shoelace grazes on the horizon. Up and down the dusty road,
teenagers play their chronic music—treble and bass.

My pizza is a perfect sun; my appetite, a lunar malady.
Afterwards, I plan for tomorrow: soak in the sun's golden
blasphemy; ponder the moon in its pallid socket. Go out,
go out—or stay at home to renew the treble and the bass.

Weekend

What of the pitchforked trees
and their skirts of green heat?
What of the curbed cars
whose tires stink on their axles?
In summer we call this happiness.
The sky a dome of scorched light.
And the shore. Everyone comes
from afar. Mounds of sand
look like stacks of potatoes.
A child shrieks; a bird answers.
Red-necked bathers float
on waves with distended fish.
On blankets we play games
with coins and cards. The sea
drags itself to lunch, fills up,
doubles over, and hurries off.
The sun goes in and out.
By late afternoon we get busy.
Pack up. Don't forget the magazine.
The article about a dictator's death
makes us feel a little bit better.

Curfew

No one's exempt. We go inside
to encapsulate ourselves in home.
Sheets of old newspapers offer
two choices: read them or use them
for warmth. Just as the flame weeps
for the candle the plummeting sun
must pity us. We know this: our lives
are obtuse. Our time in the light
of the bald reflective rock
has been gerrymandered. Night goes
prematurely flat as we covet the air
denied us and await repercussions.
Outside our dominion of parochial law
some say there are vineyards, some say war.

August

Despite
the fungus on the
candelabra,
a nocturne is a fruitful
deterrent to angst.

Piano —
that's a winter sound,
crisp
as snowfall at
an Alpine resort.

Central
air cools the finger
food:
crudités and spicy dips
mellowed by dipsomania.

The lawn
smolders. If you squint
hard,
you can make out the city,
vague as an un-hyped investment.

Hard
to imagine people out there
moaning
in slow-motion Spanish. If only they
were plutonium, petroleum, paper:
useful.

A slow
news day. Feel better. No one
you know
has been raped or tripped a land mine.
And the metal detectors are working
just fine.

Insomnia, Part I

This is how the night begins:
a gray wolf howls in the inner ear,
a horned owl hoots in the ganglia.

Craving meat, my consciousness
tracks its prey to a memory
of Oregon Basin highway construction
where a flagman waved me on
to a great fat moment of chicken fried steak.
Who could sleep, recalling this?

How I need my Neruda! My peek
into the women's changing room
deep in the wilderness of snug desire.

Instead I get the Spanish guitarist
preening taut strings next door
to the rhythm of dripping candle wax,
stalking the music of love
in the corners of his motel room.
No wonder I can not sleep.

O my patience! — hands folded, wrists bound,
captive audience to his encore
as midnight traffic applauds.

Sleep, so elusive, conceals itself
in the bristles of a wet toothbrush or
entwines the pipes in a hollow wall or
slips out thinly under the door.
What have I done to deserve this?

Insomnia, Part VII

So modern an experience no millet farmer
of the first continent could even imagine
while he babied eroding dirt for a harvest
during hours as yet too novel to possess
their own distinguishing numbers
then dropped heavily into straw or pelts
or some other archaic bedding
with whatever dreams accompany subsistence
             However
I being semi-detached from physical labor
and completely alien to agriculture and I
living bountifully with reference to
neither dawn nor dusk in some edifice
that collects insects twenty-four hours
in its warm and attractive machinery
pursue objectives which can perhaps
be retracted but never truly deleted
             And so
I yoke enervation to spectacular innovation
of little consequence and till the pliable landscape
of frequently altered programs
to improve myself while upholding
an architecture of undifferentiated time
which I would have noticed had already fallen
if only there were windows
and the plugs had been pulled.

Insomnia, Part IX

I have mastered the elongation of time.
Horizontal is my orientation, my verbatim.
You think you are walking in bed
wearing a bad prescription. You cannot
awaken from arrhythmia, nor sleep
through assembled fears. Sheep
have been my ridiculous emblem,
but these days you count only grandchildren.
I invite you to consider the marsupial
in which the young sleep soundly.
How many centuries since your ancestors
set fire to their rest and chartered
newfound light to last until dawn?
I was there in the space between baobabs,
dressed in infallible nostrils and teeth,
there to witness the fumigation
of grievances against your own nature.
Your torment is the retroactive hours
of Prudhoe Bay or Tierra del Fuego.
In between, on Route 40 West,
you bisect the lackadaisical scenery:
longhorn steer or long red mesa.
This highway was built for wide states,
for you to contemplate inopportune
vegetation tangled in your thoughts.
I flatten the view to your prognosis:
California! Every night I hear you
banging that wall you call the sea.

Insomnia, Part XII

No snow is not news, so we ingest the pill of television
and live weatherless. Beside me you lie in silhouette,
a thick book fallen from your hands, a bookmark jimmied
from its tired pages. Within inches I bypass pornography
and settle into an algorithm of dissembled sleep. Beware
my sharpened feet. I am like a man born with nine fingers,
my shame longstanding and secular, my insomnia a sulking
tributary through orchards of damaged asymmetrical fruit.
It's true, we cohabit but no longer collude. Before dropping
off, you were reading how minstrels once drew inspiration
from lovers beneath summer apple trees and their intimate
exigencies during winter storms. In the dark I wheedle time
for its slow whistle of expenditure. If not for medication
I might sing for you, as courtly and tender as a single flute.

Lorazepam

At last my compulsions
have been dismantled.

I no longer read labels sewn
into garments by famished hands,

nor sense intimations of tragedy
in maudlin workmanship.

My wants clear of residue, my roots
firmly planted in the quotidian,

I sleep better now and drink
unfiltered water devoid of ice.

The streets are suddenly empty of snow
which shall never fall again at this latitude,

but the oddities of meteorology
have ceased to disturb me.

Indifferent to the arrival time
of furious mythical horsemen,

I ride an evening commuter line that trots
like a stallion over planks and rails.

Recently my home has taken on
the contours of a thumbnail sketch.

My mate appears, for all the world,
to be a bipedal woman in her prime.

My children crouch in their playthings
beneath my level of apprehension.

With newly acquired prudence, I offer
solace to my eldest daughter:

Don't worry, sweetheart, everyone bleeds.

Extinction

The girl competes for hair color while the boy
wears black among the robins. She's a composite
of honorable mentions and a quick blouse
snatched from a laundry line. His heartache stems
from the senseless Alpine height of athletes.
These little anarchies grind their teeth, their nights
like a memory of screed. In time they meet,
they mate, passing an invoice from hand to hand.
With skin mollified by topical cream, they lose
the smoke other animals sense. The first fish
to waddle upon the sand could almost smell
the iron forge and the hooks forthcoming.
The last descendant of girl and boy is sure to be
a ruthless angler who dies when the rivers run out.

The Anthropic Principle

In our only viable universe we elbow
and crowd, and attract silver metals,
and grasp the rungs of ladders molded

for opposable thumbs. Binocular vision
facilitates our longing for birds in flight
and our fear of onrushing traffic

while mouths extract three-dimensional
succulence from even the oddest of edible
fruits. Smearing a napkin with papaya

juice, we say, *Your lover is lovely
and perhaps good.* Her necklace seems
to observe us, jewels alert, silver teeth

set in a grin or a grimace. She signals yes
or no, approach or go, but remains our only
source of tender birds and cruel traffic. Seen

through a monotheistic window, the moon
pretends to be flat and unloved. The more
distant planets live hard lives complicated

by ammonia. Just as our young crave cheap
American chocolate, our ears are compelled
to fashion adagios from January wind. Four

walls are an ideal fit for our noisy quartet
of limbs. And the rooms in which all of us
dwell have been carefully wired for sound.

Ordeal of the Bitter Water

...let the hair of the woman's head go loose...
Old Testament (Numbers 5:18)

Moses the messenger had put it in writing: the jealousy,
the double standard. When a husband had doubts,
whose wife had vowed to bear the genetic children
he wanted, the priest on duty said: *Bring the woman
and your unaltered meal.* Lucky man, the husband,
with a surplus of barley to smoke on the altar.
Dust enough from the tabernacle floor intermixed
with the single variety of water that could ruin
a woman, passing through. The wife held tight
the offering. A dampened scroll was involved.
Whatever she swore to, they believed she was akin
to sand—dispersive, instinctive, rather than clever.
They even thought she saw the stars as little suns
as warm as this one. At last, she swallowed a multitude
of ex-raindrops. Though a female may be tested and tested,
a womb is not a thigh. Let the woman's hair fly free.
And if she proves to be undefiled, her body shall revert
to a flume of release for more husbands, more priests.

Visitation

Shake the rain from your clothes before entering this room. Sit in a chair; submit to the drudgery. Sit in a chair and await detonation. Consider now your many regrets: failing to park your shoes on a doormat; feeding bread to invincible pigeons; discussing alternatives with the surgeon, then forgetting each one in an instant. Outside, the sky spills a rainbow of grease upon a restaurant known for cheap Oriental lunch. Your car squats in the brick shadow of an abandoned school in which alert pupils once glowed with an amber glow. Half-awake in a sturdy chair yet half-asleep in a stiff-legged moment of tedium, you finger the sleeves of your own fatigue. There is someone else in this room, ticking, wrapped in a thin husk of cotton folded into the umbra of electronics. Who is that figure lying there as frail as disposable chopsticks? Who is that man in bed with a plastic fuse blooming from his punctured throat?

Poland, 1990

Krakow slumbers, Bytom glows.
In between lies quiescent land,
soft and hushed
like the cloakroom of a synagogue.

Listen for the flat faint voice
of the camp survivor who chanted
kaddish at the lip of a burial pit,
or the one who spoke of vermin stench
impounded in the walls,
or the inmate intellectual
who interpreted dreams of warm shoes.

The tales have all been told,
scraped from aged vocal chords
like cinnamon from the laurel tree
or scrawled in arthritic calligraphy.

And still this earth responds
to dung with greenery.
A beast of burden drags a plough
through superstitious fields,
but shuns the fallow ground
around the camp museum.

Emeritus

I am, some might say, a vessel of travails,
a repository, cybersecure, of culture and status
reports. I remember the hoop skirt and savings
banks, the fraudulent tonics and numbers
transposed. Something akin to rebar inside me
dares not bend. Refractory, some might say.
The committee thinks with its cilia, whose members
have abandoned their sons at ballfields. Aware
of the cost differential, my industry prefers apology
to amends. In the breakroom, with its purring
thermostat and packets of salt, colleagues accrete
to me. Someone walks in with a price-biting
cheesecake. After the party, one by one they grasp
my hand, then station me next to the kill switch.

Debris

The smoke won't clear, nor the waters
recede: the sixteenth calamity
this month — a record.

Fences and turnstiles have toppled,
reverting to sour metal
in a reservoir of mud and glass.

Ashes quiver in the updraft;
soggy textiles plug the drains.
A man wearing hip boots

and a surgical mask carries
a sack full of thumbprints.
Folded up in his wallet is

a slip of paper with a series
of smeared numbers corresponding
to relatively happy people

who exist where earth and sky
enjoy sovereignty and only
sunlight falls on one's face.

Someday he will go there, after
restoring the skyline, the tree
line, the laws of nature,

thus proving himself
indispensable, as his alcoholic
mother always claimed when

he dabbed her elbows, steadied
her finances, and snapped her
memory back from the storm.

The Sherman Anti-Trust Act

You are a person
whom the American Sugar Refining Company
gave the right to thrive.
You are a person
but not a construct of fat and fingernails, a noun
with unique skin, your face a thousand truck bays,
automated doors, whose concrete teeth
in turnpike grass are embedded in the gums of economy.
You are a person
whose clean fleet of cars we are enjoined from slandering.
We believe
in your stated aims to minimize ultraviolet and pragmatize
our common bounty.
We believe,
on our greatest lakes and rivers, your touch refrains
from empirical damage.
We believe
in your broadcast arias, your libretto of claims
on wide screens and narrow.
You are a person,
not a rumor of stunned cows, nor an enterprise to sandblast
serial numbers, nor explosive machines in deep storage
now that so many men and women have fewer limbs
than balance requires.
You are a person
whose eyes see through the eyes of state legislatures,
with an ear to the ground for its hiss of multiple fuels,
with a hand in rerouting icebergs to facilitate shipping.
You are a person,

not a party complained of, not a microchip lodged
in our secret petition.
You are a person
discussed in print but immune to libel, engendering
trust and anti-trust.

Epistle of COVID-19

In recombination I keep getting born into your body,
that orphanage. I turn and turn, restless in the dank
dormitories of your lungs. You are such a pungent
eukaryote, breath like cheese, an index finger to your
lips, those doors ajar. Here you are, gun-less at last,
flourishing on mechanical ventilation. My girth
goes on doubling on ferries of blood as I write my
immigrant story into non-essential personnel. I have eyes,
you know, constructed from star-like haplotypes. And
I hear things: How you blame the bats in their night-beat
for befriending the Hubei poor. Long after onset, you can't
go back to some hut on the bank of a narrow river carving
a valley of quarantine. Let me speak frankly in cellular
whisper. Who are you to rue my exponential spread?

Ampersand

To the best of my knowledge, Ampersand
is the capital of a former Soviet republic,
a pale city of box-like buildings —
Wilmington, Delaware of the Moslem East.
From a distance, the visitor anticipates
onion domes & minarets, perhaps
a single tucked synagogue, rather than
twentieth-century concrete & remnants
of looted merchandise in the streets.
At a place called the "Sheep Market,"
jewelry & textiles are sold.
One stall features threadbare towels
for use as tourniquets. Prostheses
are also prominent goods. An imam
asks directions to the madrasa
from a former policeman who smokes
with a tailor of artisanal rags.
A siren wails for the setting sun.

From what I know, Ampersand
is a city whose citizens hope
for an extra tuber from their gardens
& for a less anemic mayor.
At noon the sun betrays them,
producing muzzle flash between
the mulberry leaves while factories
fabricate lubricants for vandalized
machines. In the midst of their elders,
boys invent chaotic games with balls

& sticks & scraps of military steel.
At intervals, prayers emerge
from unswept rooftops & blue-
tiled rooms, from barracks,
from conscripts & volunteers,
from every aperture of a city
whose shortage of conjunctions
its language can ill afford.

Friendship 7

[Transcription of John Glenn's Flight Communications (February 28, 1962)]

Not long before me there was a dog
And I sometimes wonder, Cape Flight,
What she made of her encasement.
Through these clouds I see only Wednesday.
Cape, I'm banging in and out. I recall
My training and my last real lunch.

Reading you 5 square, Cape, though
This craft is infested with sibilants.
Yes, I will override the 05g switch.
I will, if you wish, retract the scope.
Cape, my wife is beautiful when she
Rotates manually about her y-axis.

Going fly-by-wire. This is not easy
When faith in another may not be jettisoned.
And I can't help thinking of the up-range
Destroyer. Cape, do you believe in God?
Out here the void is speckled, I think,
With an old man's radiation.

Kicking in and out of orientation.
It's how I imagine the 3-foot waves
At the landing site as a lumpy mattress
Of hydrogen. Cape, is that affirm?

I've got nothing but an alloy's fingers
Holding tight to the landing bag.

Cape, I'm through the peak g now
Which feels nothing like an equation.
The capsule is flaming like a boy's
Science project. Altimeter off the peg.
I will follow your voice to a zero angle
Returning this shell to a mothering sea.

Airport

A man with pistol and stammer
flowers at the head of a queue of women
dressed for sleeplessness,

the crush
of shoeless feet as quiet
as a submarine drowning.

Strangled luggage wheels past TVs
where sex is less
than two feet tall

and grandmothers worship
the Virgin
imprinted on grilled cheese.

For passengers half out of their clothes
the lapidary shops amuse
while children savor their own tongues.

Time chafes.
Here it is neither light
nor lightlessness.

From red-eyed runways
silver pods rise above
skunk cabbage, cattails, a marsh of brine.

This is a way to transport flesh and leather,
to convey beyond clouds
the years of rain within us.

The Monroe Doctrine

Once, we loved oceans for their privacy.
Cuba was a dust cloud of allergens.
The Marines had vacated Santo Domingo

but left behind ominous candy wrappers.
In Nueva York I was eleven and alive
with playground aftershocks. Icicles

framed stairwell windows. Haitians
were moving in with their soft language.
Winter was safe as a snoring grandfather.

In North Carolina the Marines lived
glumly and stirred only in the greatest
heat. According to our president—the first

from Texas—the tapered tips of Asia
were connected to us by promises
in deep green camouflage. They say

even this cup I drink from is made
of petroleum. To "anxious and interested
spectators," every land is holy. Lacking pilots

our aircraft suckle on circuitry in the space
above a province of Pakistan. Now we awaken
every time a Parisian coughs in his sleep.

Christmas Eve

Now is the hour for a sentimental car crash.
To stay warm, police agitate themselves
as though waiting for biopsy. On a hardened lawn
reindeer tilt, lame in their wire legs, their electric
tongues unfit for discourse between the living
and never-have-lived. The emergency team
seems worthy with their passion for making
space. Here comes the body, who could be the real
Jesus, more so than he with a lightbulb behind
his plastic head. They extract him glove-handed
through metal and beautiful platters of glass. Physics
begins to rain, delightful wet spectra derived
from reflections of ambulance lights. In the morning
a neighbor's child will discover silver in the street.

The Homestead Act

During the years of starvation
rations, the ground is hard,
and all are ploughless, the young
winnowed to weasel bones.
In 1862 no one's more tragic
than a pioneer with cataracts.
None remain now to "sell said land
for the benefit of said infants,"
but a few reached the coast
to show their kids a circus
of water and whales. It's hard
to decline the eighty-acre panorama
in favor of Our Lady of Guadalupe,
to eschew cattle and the amplitude
of their defecations on the outskirts
of creosote country north
of the Magellanic Clouds.
The General Land Office
keeps the camps for emigrants
at three degrees microwave.
At the checkpoint they clamor
for tepid water and dream of yachts
on the Rio Grande. It's the waiting,
the terrible waiting, as if for surgery
on the eyes with a local anesthetic.
Meanwhile, fighting continues
at Shiloh, the war not nearly won.

Surplus

Take a seat anywhere. We have more house
than we need. More driveway width, more
plywood, more squirrels in the impacted trees.
More water from the showerhead, in the wading
pool, in the gutters draining to nowhere.
Lately, I've accepted more phone calls
from loquacious mechanisms. When I read
the news online, I find equivocations
by the Federal Communications Commission.
More medical reports on asymptomatic conditions.
More liver spots and kwashiorkor, more redheads
ashamed, more salons. Despite maps to everywhere,
there are more secret routes to the mattress store.
Fewer bells, more alarms. An increase in orders
of restraint and protection. No more tigers, but more
photographs of tigers. When occupants squirm
in refugee camps, they relocate the axis of the world.
The relentless correlation between more fire,
less forest. So many wedding rings lost
in restrooms. Fewer wait staff, longer waits
for tannic acid, foam-topped beer, real orange flavor.
More light when asleep. More embargo and animus.
Fewer varieties of organisms, but more eyeballs
on advertisements. More lightning with
or without rain, more rain with or without
thunder, more thunder with or without weather.
Everyone admires Vera Rubin who disclosed
more material for the universe to eat. Now
we know three-dimensional space is a walk-in
closet in which any number of us may cower.

Breathe

As expected, I see astral phenomena when my life
unmoors from that tidal clock we call the moon.
These people, however, won't leave me to my drift.
While shoving in staccato, they infuse me
with a canister of chemical stimulant channeled
through a durable transparent bag. Because ribs
are a great inconvenience, they impose upon me
new hematomas. I am a tantrum restrained by a fat
knee. It's worse than wet socks, worse than libido
losing traction. What are their criteria for this assault
which simplifies me to a replica of myself? I ride
green waves of gag reflex. The air tastes rubbery
as if tainted by latex. In this place, they follow strict
protocol: Wash hands. Or anyone you touch may die.

A Soul of Few Words

after Wislawa Szymborska

The soul, born of approximate lust,
can not differentiate arm from leg
as it puckers without ulterior motive.

The soul is schooled in the use of knees
to stake its claim to space and motion
while unaware of its own dichotomy.

The soul kicks to express discomfort,
kicks the back of the seat in front of it,
kicks an empty can down a frozen alley.

The soul cranes its neck to observe
the maximum number of yellow bikinis
while long-necked cranes pass overhead.

The soul, which marries late in life,
eventually loses track of its mate yet
abandons the onerous task of singularity.

The soul lives among laconic draperies
and muted shades of old upholstery
that complement its many lies of omission.

The soul, which chafes in its aging skin and
worries about leaving the world intestate,
shuffles to the bathroom every half-hour.

The soul hardens, thaws, reconstitutes
into a lesser hairless thing that throbs
in its daily harness of nutritional intake.

The souls murmurs itself to sleep
believing no one has ever heard it
disclosing secrets to a faithful pillow.

Fourteen Lines or Less

Outdated as a daiquiri, she enters the world's
great ballroom where the carnage of envy
orbits her form. She is smart in two ways,
minimum. Lightly glazed, her poise unspools
serendipity, shunning golden sponsorships.
What she is not is a surgical mask nor
a soldiers' white memorial. Perhaps she's akin
to the obdurate cardiac routine which exists
in a field of charge and discharge.
Under the feckless stars, under the trees
of unison, lovers refer to her once, then
silence. She deposes discussion like literature
deeply felt. She can say this in fourteen lines
or less like a lyric poem with a smooth neck.

Bread

after Michael Jones, *Leningrad: State of Siege*

Bread was bread, then bread was flax, then bread was a leather belt. In September the storehouse went up from the Junkers. Dogs and cats disappeared like martyred children on the Lychkovo train. One night the Wehrmacht bombed the zoo; the elephant died without bread. Zhdanov stayed fat writing loudspeaker doctrine at Canteen No. 12. An architect lived on pigeons trapped in a cupola. Bread was carpenters glue; bread was horsehide soup. Lips grew darker and stuck to the teeth.

I was resting at the Anichkov Bridge—the icy Fontanka like a confection—on a pile of snow seasoned with corpses. I was resting into an exothermal death when a girl in a sundress tugged me to her mother on firewatch who fed me inedible cellulose. Bread was dust shaken from a flour sack. Bread was swept from the floor. We were warmed by one square meter of wood and quenched our thirst with buckets from wounds in the Neva. Tea was water and salt.

In the spring bread became broth made from nettles and dandelion roots. Only our diaries put on weight. In August, though, spouses stopped sniping. Starving ballerinas straightened their shoulders. An academic finished his treatise on the cabbage moth. The Hermitage drew a little power from the Baltic Fleet to pollinate symposia. Sheet metal workers philosophized. A seamstress I knew learned Greek. At the Philharmonic Eliasberg with a palsied baton conducted a symphony for bread in C major. The orchestra played through its bones, music like shutters opening to the sunny smell of a baker's wares.

The Greenland Vikings

The Greenland Vikings wandered far from home,
conquering their head colds,
driven by an appetite for wood.
Their sleep was flat and leaden like the sea;
their wives were calm and broken in.

Your sleep is small and greedy
as the autumn squirrel.
Upon our rooftop acorns thump,
alluding to the presence
of good timber in the dark.

From trees of great distinction
Norsemen built their ships and sailed
until all waves devoured themselves
and even Viking marriages dissolved.

Only dreams propel you now — windswept,
overlapping like layers of the sky.
I know this: for I feel you rotate
on your feather pillow, feel you spin
as if within a nightmare
of that shocking round world
where shipwrecked Vikings
raged beyond words.

Theory of Everything

Imagine a point of light, the hothouse of creation,
colorless, odorless, prisoner of destiny.
As the universe acquires an inflated sense of self,
high-energy particles marry, quarrel, divorce.
After a while stars accrete.
The Earth grows a fire in its belly.
Finally it rains.

From acidic oceans with a carbon tang,
fishes born with Darwinian nostrils
sniff oxygen in the air. Wet-legged
species wallow in mud while continents
marry, quarrel, divorce.

Using stone and wood, hominids learn
to nullify the speed and strength of prey
and sift nutrition from the furry earth
in which they inter the honored dead
shrouded in myths, imaginary deeds.
Clans intermarry, quarrel, divorce.

Osiris takes over.
Yahweh takes over.
Zeus takes over.
Allah takes over.
His Holiness raises a papal fist,
but the spoils of war devolve to the Doge,
then to the Khan who stumbles into empire
and stubs his bloody toes.

The nobility mingles recessive genes.
Mariners ply the seas for celebrity, souls and gold
as monarchs inflict enlightened wounds.
The scabs of extinction are picked for oil and coal
by nations that marry, quarrel, divorce.
To escape the phosgene flood,
survivors take flight on canvas wings.

Today the affluent carp and cajole
while heavily pigmented children
weaken in a field of flies. We know
the digitized voices/images
of men sporting radioactive holsters
overflowing with unstable atoms
that marry, quarrel, divorce.

Think how space itself is curved
like the surface of this particular globe.
Who knows? If you travel fast enough,
you may meet your maker, and your maker's maker.
Or, in a fit of anthropoid rage, you may
set fire to your parents' homes, burning them
down before you were born, before
they married, quarreled, divorced.

Yet here you culminate, lit by Edison's profitable light.
Wearing Josephine's nose, the hair of Cleopatra,
the hands of the mistress of a Hebrew king,
you plead for a promise from me that we will
never marry, never quarrel, never divorce.

Acknowledgments

Many of the poems in this collection first appeared in the following publications:

Bayou Magazine ("My Wife Is Shrinking")
Arcadia ("Late Summer")
Connecticut River Review ("Lot's Wife" and "Visitation")
FutureCycle Poetry ("Hurricane")
The Cape Rock ("The Donor")
A Different Latitude ("Geriatrics")
Slant ("Enemy")
The Philadelphia Inquirer ("Pockets")
Phoebe ("La Tienda Mexicana" and "Curfew")
Fourteen Hills: The SFSU Review ("Akhmatova #4")
Wavelength ("Akhmatova #6" and "The Engine")
Cadillac Cicatrix ("Akhmatova #10")
Visions-International ("Kaddish")
Oberon ("New Jersey, or Somewhere")
Ozone Park Journal ("Another Fraudulent Memoir")
Lady Jane's Miscellany ("Impression: Sunday")
Argestes ("Death by Pizza" and "Debris")
Bluestem ("Weekend")
Freshwater ("August")
Stray Dog ("Insomnia, Part I")
Clockhouse ("Insomnia, Part VII")
Caesura ("Insomnia, Part IX")
Wisconsin Review ("Insomnia, Part XII")
San Pedro River Review ("Lorazepam")
Southword ("Extinction")
The New Poet ("The Anthropic Principle")

Poems & Plays ("Poland, 1990")
Cardinal Sins ("Emeritus")
Beloit Poetry Journal ("The Sherman Anti-Trust Act")
Consequence Magazine ("Ampersand")
Soundings East ("Friendship 7")
Jabberwock Review ("The Monroe Doctrine")
River Styx ("Christmas Eve")
Water-Stone Review ("Surplus")
Lullwater Review ("Breathe")
Blood and Honey Review ("A Soul of Few Words")
Isthmus ("Fourteen Lines or Less")
North American Review ("Bread")
Poems That Thump in the Dark/Second Glance ("The Greenland Vikings")
Nedge ("Theory of Everything")